Visual Geography Series®

GREECE

...in Pictures

Prepared by
Geography Department

Lerner Publications Company
Minneapolis

Independent Picture Service

**The walled Monastery of Saint John, founded in the
eleventh century, overlooks the island of Patmos.**

This book is an all-new edition of the Visual Geography Series. Previous editions were published by
Sterling Publishing Company, New York City. The
text, set in 10/12 Century Textbook, is fully revised
and updated, and new photographs, maps, charts, and
captions have been added.

LIBRARY OF CONGRESS CATALOGING-IN-PUBLICATION DATA

Greece— in pictures / prepared by Geography Department,
  Lerner Publications Company.
    p. cm. — (Visual geography series)
  Rev. ed. of: Greece in pictures / by Robert V. Masters.
  Includes index.
  Summary: Describes the topography, history, society,
economy, and government of Greece
  ISBN 0-8225-1882-0 (lib. bdg.)
  1. Greece—Juvenile literature. [1. Greece.] I. Masters,
Robert V., 1914-   Greece in pictures. II. Lerner
Publications Company. Geography Dept. III. Series: Visual
geography series
DF17.G787   1992
949.5—dc20   91-23302

International Standard Book Number: 0-8225-1882-1
Library of Congress Catalog Card Number: 91-23302

VISUAL GEOGRAPHY SERIES®

Publisher
Harry Jonas Lerner
Associate Publisher
Nancy M. Campbell
Senior Editor
Mary M. Rodgers
Editors
Gretchen Bratvold
Tom Streissguth
Photo Researcher
Bill Kauffmann
Editorial/Photo Assistants
Marybeth Campbell
Colleen Sexton
Consultants/Contributors
Theofanis G. Stavrou
Sandra K. Davis
Designer
Jim Simondet
Cartographer
Carol F. Barrett
Indexers
Kristine I. Spangard
Sylvia Timian
Production Manager
Gary J. Hansen

Independent Picture Service

**Sponge sellers are a common sight in many Greek towns
and cities.**

Acknowledgments

Title page photo by Drs. A. A. M. van der Heyden,
Naarden, the Netherlands

Elevation contours adapted from *The Times Atlas of
the World*, seventh comprehensive edition (New York:
Times Books, 1985).

2 3 4 5 6 7 8 9 10 – JR – 04 03 02 01 00 99 98 97 96

This famous sculpture of the fifth century B.C., entitled Discobolus (the discus thrower), depicts an ancient Olympic athlete. The contests of discus throwing, wrestling, running, boxing, and javelin throwing have remained as competitive events in the modern Olympic Games.

Courtesy of Terme Museum, Rome

Contents

Introduction **5**

1) The Land **7**
Topography. Rivers. Climate. Flora and Fauna. Natural Resources. Athens. Secondary Cities.

2) History and Government **19**
Minoans and Mycenaeans. Oligarchs and Tyrants. Athens and Sparta. Greece and Rome. The Byzantine Empire. The Ottoman Conquest. The War for Independence. The Greek Kingdom. World War I and the Postwar Crisis. World War II. Political Turmoil and Dictatorship. Recent Events. Government

3) The People **39**
Ethnic Identity and Language. Health and Education. Literature. Visual Arts. Religion and Festivals. Food. Sports and Recreation.

4) The Economy **50**
Manufacturing. Agriculture. Mining and Fishing. Trade and Shipping. Tourism. Energy and Transportation. The Future.

Index **64**

MACEDONIA
BULGARIA
TURKEY
Istanbul
(Constantinople)
Bosporus St.

ALBANIA

Axios R.
Strymon R.
Kavalla
Thessaloniki
THASOS
SAMOTHRACE
Thermaic Gulf

Drakolimni
Pinios R.
Larissa
LEMNOS
TROY
(Ruins)

CORFU
Igoumenitsa

IONIAN
ISLANDS

Volos
Volos G.
SKIATHOS
SKOPELOS
SKYROS

AEGEAN SEA
S P O R A D E S

TURKEY

LESBOS

Izmir
(Smyrna)

ITHACA
Acheloos R.
Pinios R.
DELPHI
(Ruins)
Thebes
G. of Euboea
EUBOEA
CHIOS

I S L A N D S

SAMOS

Gulf of Patras
Gulf of Corinth
Patras
Kalavrita
Corinth
(Ruins)
Corinth Canal
ATHENS
Marathon
Marathon Dam
Piraeus

OLYMPIA
(Ruins)
MYCENAE
(Ruins)
Alpheios R.

ZAKYNTHOS

IONIAN SEA

Saronic Gulf
Cape
Sounion

Hydra
HYDRA

MYKONOS
DELOS
PATMOS

KALYMNOS

CYCLADES
IS.

NAXOS

D O D E C A N E S E

KOS

Rhodes

Sparta
Eurotas R.

Pylos
(Navarino)

*Gulf of
Laconia*

SANTORINI
Thira

I S.

RHODES

MEDITERRANEAN SEA

GREECE

N
↑

- - - - - Regional Boundaries

——— Major Roads

| 0 | 50 | 100 Miles |
| 0 | 50 | 100 Kilometers |

CRETE
Iraklion
KNOSSOS
(Ruins)

EUROPE
GREECE

| 0 | 400 Miles |
| 0 | 400 Kilometers |

Arctic Circle
20°
0°
20°

NORWEGIAN
SEA

60°

NORTH
ATLANTIC
OCEAN

20°

40°

MEDITERRANEAN SEA
0°
20°
40°

METRIC CONVERSION CHART
To Find Approximate Equivalents

WHEN YOU KNOW:	MULTIPLY BY:	TO FIND:
AREA		
acres	0.41	hectares
square miles	2.59	square kilometers
CAPACITY		
gallons	3.79	liters
LENGTH		
feet	30.48	centimeters
yards	0.91	meters
miles	1.61	kilometers
MASS (weight)		
pounds	0.45	kilograms
tons	0.91	metric tons
VOLUME		
cubic yards	0.77	cubic meters
TEMPERATURE		
degrees Fahrenheit	0.56 (*after* subtracting 32)	degrees Celsius

This small shop in Athens, the capital of Greece, offers a variety of household objects and folk crafts.

Introduction

The Hellenic Republic, or Greece, has been an independent nation since the early nineteenth century. Greek civilization, however, is at least 5,000 years old. Ancient Greeks developed the earliest democratic governments, invented many branches of science and mathematics, and wrote some of the world's first plays and history books. These works and ideas created a foundation for modern European culture.

The first inhabitants of Greece settled in the country's northern mountains and on the islands of the Aegean Sea. The region's rugged terrain hindered communication and cooperation among the ancient Greek cities. The result was economic rivalry and frequent civil wars. Militarily weak and politically divided, the Greeks became easy prey for more powerful empires in southern Europe and Asia.

Ottoman Turks from Asia Minor (modern Turkey) conquered most of Greece by the sixteenth century. For 400 years, while the Turks maintained control, Greece remained isolated and poor. In the 1820s, with the help of several powerful European countries, parts of Greece won independence. Although Greece and Turkey now share a common boundary, tension and mistrust still exist between them.

Despite their successful fight for independence, Greeks have struggled to earn a living from their country's limited productive land. Many Greeks have emigrated, while Greek leaders have searched for ways to promote economic growth. In 1981, for example, Greece became a member of the European Union (EU), an association of western European nations that follow common trade policies. As trade barriers fall between EU countries, EU membership should bring increased export earnings and new investment to Greek companies.

Despite the efforts of its government, Greece continues to face serious economic problems. The overall standard of living for Greeks is low compared to that of many other European nations. While taking pride in their nation's ancient past, the Greeks must prepare their industries for tougher competition with the rest of Europe in the future.

For protection from invading armies, many Greek monasteries were built on remote and unreachable heights. This monastery is perched on the peninsula of Mount Athos, an independent religious state in the region of Macedonia.

This rural road passes through an olive grove in a valley of southern Greece. Farmers use much of the country's level land for the cultivation of fruit and olive trees.

Courtesy of Greek National Tourist Organization

Hotels and restaurants line the small harbor of Hydra, the largest town on the island of Hydra. Popular with foreign tourists, Hydra has also become a favorite location for artists, writers, and filmmakers.

1) The Land

Greece occupies the southernmost part of the Balkan Peninsula in southeastern Europe. With a total land area of 50,961 square miles, Greece is slightly larger than the state of Louisiana. About 20 percent of Greek territory is made up of widely scattered islands in the seas that lie to the east, west, and south of the mainland.

In the north, Greece shares borders with the Balkan nations of Albania, the republic of Macedonia, and Bulgaria. Turkey lies along the eastern shore of the Aegean Sea. An arm of the Mediterranean Sea, the Aegean stretches from northern Greece

to Crete, the country's largest and southernmost island. Off the mainland's western coast is the Ionian Sea, which separates Greek territory from southern Italy.

Topography

Mountains dominate the landscape of mainland Greece, much of which consists of rocky terrain and thin, infertile soil. The highlands hinder overland travel between many towns and villages. Since transportation by sea is easier in many regions, most large Greek towns lie on natural harbors

Melting snow supplies water to Drakolimni (Dragon Lake), the largest of several seasonal lakes in the Pindus Mountains. Many of these lakes dry up in the heat and drought of the summer.

Photo by Ioannis Epaminondas

or in the lowlands near the coasts. The islands of the Aegean and Ionian seas are actually the peaks of undersea mountains. The geological activity that created the islands continues to cause earthquakes throughout the country.

MAINLAND GREECE

Rugged, isolated highlands lie along Greece's long northern border. In the northeastern region of Thrace, these uplands end in marshes and lagoons along the Aegean coast. Thrace, a sparsely populated area, shares a short land frontier with Turkey to the east.

West of Thrace are the fertile river basins and rolling uplands of the Macedonia region. The foothills of the Pindus Mountains straddle Greece's borders with the republic of Macedonia and Albania. Epirus, a remote region of northwestern Greece, is cut off from the rest of the country by the Pindus range. Only a few major roads cross these highlands, which reach 8,000 feet in altitude.

The Pindus Mountains continue southward as far as the Gulfs of Patras and Corinth. These busy shipping channels divide central Greece and the Peloponnesus, a large peninsula of steep mountains, rocky capes, and narrow river valleys. Boeotia and Attica occupy another peninsula that extends southeastward from central Greece and ends at Cape Sounion. Attica, the most densely populated region of the country, consists of small mountain ranges divided by flat, fertile basins. Industrial centers and ports line the western coast of Attica along the Saronic Gulf. North of Attica, the Gulf of Euboea forms a narrow strait between the coast of Boeotia and the island of Euboea.

North of the Gulf of Euboea stretches the wide, low-lying plain of Thessaly. The Greeks drained marshes along the Pinios River to create Thessaly's fertile farmland. Most road and rail routes between northern and southern Greece pass through Thessaly near the Gulf of Volos, a sheltered harbor. Mount Olympus (9,570 feet), the highest peak in Greece, rises near the Aegean coast between northern Thessaly and Macedonia.

THE ISLANDS

There are four main island groups in Greece. Off the country's western coast are the Ionian Islands, which include Corfu, Ithaca, and Zakynthos. The Cyclades, the most populous island group, extend southeastward from Attica. Passenger and cargo ferries connect Naxos, Mykonos, Santorini, and the other Cyclades to the Greek capital city of Athens.

The Dodecanese Islands form a long chain in the southeastern Aegean off the coast of Turkey. Although its name means "twelve islands," the Dodecanese contains two dozen inhabited islands and many smaller, uninhabited islets. Fruit and olive groves thrive in the mild climate and fertile soil of Rhodes, the largest of the Dodecanese. The islands of Kalymnos,

Thira, a town on the island of Santorini, lies on the rim of a volcanic crater. Many buildings on Santorini and on other Greek islands are built of whitewashed stone.

The marble figures of the Terrace of the Lions on Delos, an island in the Cyclades group, guard an area that the ancient Greeks considered sacred.

The Pinios River in Thessaly flows through a thriving agricultural region. After World War II (1939–1945), the Greek government built a modern highway along the Pinios. The new road cut travel time between northern and southern Greece.

Kos, and Patmos are home to a decreasing population of fishermen and farmers.

The Sporades are scattered across the northern Aegean Sea from the shores of Thessaly to Turkey. Lesbos, Chios, and Samos are remote and mountainous islands in the eastern Aegean. Off the coast of Thrace lie Thasos and Samothrace.

Crete—the country's largest and most mountainous island—has a series of high ranges that tower above the plains that line its northern and southern coasts. Mount Ida (8,060 feet), near the island's center, is Crete's highest point. Large groves of orange and olive trees are common in Crete's mountain valleys and coastal lowlands.

Rivers

Rivers flow in the mountains and lowlands of Greece, but the country's waterways are not navigable. Most follow a short, winding course from the interior highlands to the sea. The floodplains that surround the rivers near their sea outlets, especially in Macedonia and Thessaly, provide fertile soil for farming.

Flowing 137 miles, the Achelous is the longest river lying entirely within Greece. The Achelous begins in the Pindus Mountains and empties into the Ionian Sea near the western end of the Gulf of Patras. The Pinios River, which also rises in the Pindus range, winds 125 miles northeastward through the plain of Thessaly before reaching the Thermaic Gulf.

Many rivers that originate in the Balkan Peninsula flow through northern Greece and then into the Aegean. After crossing the Bulgarian border, the Strymon passes through a wide valley. The Axios River, which enters Greece from the republic of Macedonia, reaches its outlet near the city of Thessaloniki.

The Eurotas River in the Peloponnesus flows southward for 60 miles and empties into the Gulf of Laconia. Farms, small towns, and the city of Sparta lie between two parallel mountain ranges in the broad Eurotas Valley. The Alpheios River in the western Peloponnesus passes Olympia, the site of the ancient Olympic Games, and flows into the Ionian Sea.

Climate

Most of Greece has a mild climate with warm, dry summers and rainy winters. Winds reaching the Greek mainland from the west bring the heaviest rainfall to the central and northern mountains. The highlands of northwestern Greece receive as much as 60 inches of precipitation annually. During winter, snow often caps the highest peaks of the Pindus.

Thessaly—an area of low elevation—is the driest and hottest part of mainland Greece. Macedonia and Thrace, regions to the north, enjoy milder weather. In Thessaloniki temperatures average 79° F in July

A windmill overlooks a village street on the island of Mykonos, one of the Cyclades Islands. Mykonos produces wine, figs, and grain, but the island's most valuable industry is tourism.

Photo by Ioannis Epaminondas

A rare snowfall dusted the Macedonian city of Thessaloniki in the winter of 1988. Snow occurs in this part of Greece about once every four years.

and August, the warmest summer months. In January, the coldest month, the city's average temperature is 43° F. Annual rainfall in Thessaloniki is about 18 inches.

Rain-bearing winds cross the central highlands and drop most of their moisture before reaching the Aegean coasts, central Greece, and the Greek islands. Regions south and east of the Pindus range have a drier climate than northern Greece. Summer skies are usually clear, and temperatures can reach 100° F. Winters are rainy and cool. Temperatures in Athens average 48° F in January and 80° F in July and August.

Dry winds from the north and northeast and cool sea breezes moderate summer temperatures in the Peloponnesus. Rainfall increases with elevation, but hot southerly winds bring drought conditions to southern Greece and most of the Aegean

Courtesy of Gretchen Bratvold

High winds on the Aegean Sea cause hazards to sailing vessels as well as damage to island vegetation, such as these twisted pines on the island of Rhodes.

islands from June or July until October. The summer drought is followed immediately by a rainy winter season. Spring is a period of mild temperatures and changeable weather throughout the country.

Flora and Fauna

A wide variety of plant life once covered the mainland and islands of Greece. Centuries of tree cutting to clear land for farming and settlement, however, have destroyed most of the country's forests. The largest remaining woodlands are in the Pindus Mountains and in the highlands of the Peloponnesus. Fir, beech, and pine trees grow on mountain slopes above 4,000 feet. Alpine lichens (mosses) and flowering plants replace these trees above 6,000 feet. Oak, beech, chestnut, maple, and elm trees

Once covered with trees, the Greek countryside has changed greatly since people settled the land. Much of rural Greece now consists of barren hills, sparse pasture, and irrigated groves of fruit trees.

Plants that can conserve water, such as this prickly pear cactus on Rhodes, thrive on the southern Aegean islands.

survive in isolated groves and river valleys. Scrub vegetation known as *maquis*—consisting of laurel, oleander, wild olives, and other low shrubs—makes hiking difficult in Greece's flat countryside and on hillsides. *Frigana,* a mixture of various plants that thrive in dry conditions, is a common ground cover in southern Greece and on the islands.

Many large mammals inhabit the remote regions of Greece. A few wild boars, black bears, and deer live in the highlands of Epirus. Wolves also exist in small numbers in the mountainous northern regions. Lynx, foxes, badgers, weasels, and the chamois—an agile, antelope-like animal—survive in northern and southern Greece. The ibex (a wild goat) also populates mountainous areas of Crete. Caves along the Greek coasts shelter a few sea lions (large seals). Hawks, pheasants, and nightingales still inhabit mainland Greece, despite the loss of many forests. Pelicans, storks, and egrets are common in large and small Greek harbors.

Although Greece suffers serious water pollution in some areas, many species of fish still inhabit the seas along the country's coast. Lobsters, shrimp, mussels, octopuses, and tuna populate fishing grounds in the Aegean and Ionian seas. Diving for sponges—fish skeletons that can absorb water—is a traditional occupation of islanders. Dolphins, although rarely seen, still survive in the Greek seas.

Natural Resources

Many centuries of mining in Greece have depleted the country's natural resources. Nevertheless, mineral deposits still benefit the country's economy. Large amounts of lignite (brown coal) exist in Macedonia, in the central Peloponnesus, and on the island of Euboea. Ninety percent of the lignite mined in Greece supplies electric power plants. Bauxite, an important component of aluminum, has also been discovered in central Greece. Other minerals present in small quantities include nickel, iron ore, sulfur, manganese, chromium, copper, and silver.

Quarries (digging sites) in Attica yield marble, an important building material used in Greece since prehistoric times. The islands of the northern Aegean also supply marble, as well as zinc, copper, and iron ore. Deposits of petroleum and natural gas lie off the coast of Thasos. These finds in the northern Aegean, however, supply only a small percentage of the country's energy requirements.

Independent Picture Service

The country's growing cities are putting a strain on Greece's scarce water resources. Frequent summer droughts worsen the situation in mainland regions and on the islands, many of which have no natural water sources. The Marathon Dam in Attica was built to supply drinking water to the capital city of Athens.

The Theater of Dionysus in Athens, constructed in the fourth century B.C., was the scene of plays, military parades, and mock naval battles.

Athens

Athens and its suburbs have a population of 3 million. The city occupies a plain in southwestern Attica near the Saronic Gulf. Low mountains rise above Athens to the north and east. Within the city are the Acropolis—the ancient fortified hill that protected early settlements—and the isolated summit of Lycabettus. Five miles to the west lies Piraeus, an industrial center and busy international port with a population of 200,000.

Athens became wealthy and powerful after its leaders formed a military alliance of Greek city-states in the fifth century

The Arch of Hadrian, a gateway built in A.D. 132 during the reign of the Roman emperor Hadrian, commemorated the Roman rule of Athens.

B.C. After a war with Sparta, Athens was conquered by the Roman Empire in the second century B.C. Later invasions from eastern and western Europe further reduced the city's size and population. The Ottoman armies of Turkey took control of Athens in the fifteenth century A.D. and held it for nearly 400 years. When the Greeks overthrew Ottoman rule in central Greece in the early 1800s, Athens became the capital of the newly established Greek republic.

The center of the Greek government and economy, Athens is also home to the National Archaeological Museum and the University of Athens, the largest Greek school of higher learning. Factories in and near the city produce ships, textiles, building materials, and chemicals. Ancient monuments and busy shopping districts attract visitors, and tourism remains a vital part of the city's economy. Industries and heavy automobile traffic, however, have caused serious air pollution. Smog is damaging historic buildings in Athens as well as the health of Athenians.

Secondary Cities

Thessaloniki (population 384,000), Greece's second largest city, stretches along a narrow inlet of the Aegean Sea. The chief commercial town of northern Greece, Thessaloniki is an important seaport and manufacturing center. Ironworks, shipyards, and textile mills are among the city's largest employers.

Founded by the Macedonians in the fourth century B.C., Thessaloniki later became a principal city of the Byzantine Empire, which controlled territory in Greece, Turkey, and the Balkan Peninsula. The Ottoman Turks occupied the city from the fifteenth century until 1912, when a large part of Macedonia joined the Greek republic. Many fine Byzantine churches survive in central Thessaloniki, but most of the city's commercial and residential buildings were built in the twentieth century.

The harbor of Patras (population 153,000), the largest city in the Peloponnesus, shelters commercial vessels and passenger ships. Turkish forces destroyed the city in the 1820s during the Greek War of Independence. After its rebuilding, Patras became a commercial and manufacturing hub with shipyards, food-processing plants,

Built in the 1430s, while Thessaloniki was under Turkish occupation, the White Tower has become the city's most famous landmark.

Independent Picture Service

Courtesy of Gretchen Bratvold

In many Greek cities, vendors set up small shops that sell a wide variety of goods to passing pedestrians.

and textile mills. The city's docks also handle agricultural exports from southern Greece.

Iraklion, with a population of 116,000, is the administrative center of Crete. The city, once an important Mediterranean port, came under Italian and Turkish occupation before Crete gained its independence in 1913. Iraklion now supports a variety of small industries and is a base for tourists exploring the island's many archaeological sites.

Volos (population 77,000), on the northern shore of the Gulf of Volos, is the chief port of Thessaly. The city has textile mills as well as tobacco and cement industries. The capital of Thessaly, Larissa (population 103,000) has been a center of grain farming since prehistoric times. Larissa still serves as a commercial center for farms in the region.

Photo by Daniel H. Condit

A sixteenth-century fortress rises above the harbor at Iraklion, Crete. Engineers from the Italian city of Venice built the fort to protect the busy port from raids by pirates and by the Ottoman Turks.

The Tholos, a round, domed building at Delphi, was raised in the fourth century B.C. Located on the slopes of Mount Parnassus in central Greece, Delphi was a place of pilgrimage for many Greeks, who visited the Delphic temples to learn their future.

2) History and Government

People have lived on the Greek mainland and islands since prehistoric times. Caves and hilltops in Epirus were the site of human settlements that date to around 10,000 B.C. Animal bones and stone weapons found at these places reveal that Stone Age Greeks hunted lions, deer, and wolves in the forests that once covered the region. The Pinios River Valley in Thessaly became a center of grain farming around 8000 B.C. Peoples who may have come from North Africa settled the Cyclades Islands and Crete as early as 3000 B.C.

By about 2500 B.C., small villages and towns were thriving in central and southern Greece. The inhabitants built thick walls around their settlements and forged bronze weapons for their defense. A busy

The Minoan kings ruled a wealthy seafaring empire from this palace at Knossos on Crete. Archaeologists who uncovered the palace in the early twentieth century rebuilt the walls and recreated many vivid Minoan paintings.

trade in obsidian—a hard volcanic rock used to make arrows and tools—developed between the Cyclades and the mainland. The people of Attica began extracting silver and lead from mines along the Aegean coast during this period.

Minoans and Mycenaeans

On Crete, trading towns and farming settlements united under the leadership of a king, who ruled from the palace of Knossos. Named after King Minos, a legendary ruler of the island, the Minoans traded with peoples in the eastern Mediterranean and developed Europe's first system of

A tourist stands underneath the Lion Gate, a part of the massive walls of ancient Mycenae.

writing. By 2000 B.C., the Minoans had colonized several islands of the Cyclades, including Santorini. Farms flourished near the island coasts, and Minoan merchants exchanged goods with North Africa and the Middle East.

Around 2000 B.C., invaders from the north conquered many settlements on mainland Greece. The newcomers established walled cities in isolated valleys and coastal areas of southern and central Greece. Mycenae, a fortified settlement in the northeastern Peloponnesus, eventually became the most powerful city in the region. Over the next few centuries, Mycenaean civilization spread to many Aegean islands and to the western coast of Asia Minor (modern Turkey).

In about 1450 B.C., a volcanic explosion on Santorini destroyed many cities in the southern Aegean. After this disaster, Minoan civilization declined, allowing the Mycenaeans to take control of Crete and other Minoan sites. The rising power of Mycenae, however, led to competition and armed conflict with other cities in the region. By the mid-1200s B.C., Mycenae and its allies were warring with Troy, a kingdom in northwestern Asia Minor. The legendary heroes of the Trojan War became important figures in ancient Greek culture and religion.

Shortly after 1200 B.C., Mycenae suffered either a natural or a military disaster that destroyed the city. Dorians from northern Greece, equipped with stronger iron weapons, then overthrew the Mycenaean kings. Many Greeks fled to remote regions of the Peloponnesus or to the coast of Asia Minor.

Following these invasions, a period of cultural and economic stagnation began. Greek settlements became more isolated, and trade decreased between Greek ports and the cities of the Middle East and Africa. In many Greek cities, the arts of sculpture, painting, and writing, which had flourished earlier, declined or were forgotten.

Oligarchs and Tyrants

As increasing numbers of Dorians arrived in southern Greece, new city-states arose. The leaders of the city-states controlled both the fortified urban centers and the surrounding land. By about 700 B.C., a powerful class of landowners had established oligarchies (rule by a small group of citizens) in Athens, Sparta, Corinth, and Thebes. The city-states maintained their independence and often fought over trade and territory. Yet the inhabitants of these towns used a common alphabet and shared a common religion. They also identified themselves with a common name—Hellenes—after an early Dorian people from Thessaly.

With increased trade and abundant harvests, the city-states began to prosper. But the growing population of Greece was

Courtesy of Museum of Fine Arts, Boston

Lion sculptures, which were ancient Greek symbols of protection, guarded the entrances to temples, homes, and palaces in the Greek city-states.

21

causing a shortage of land. In addition, discontent was growing with the oligarchs and their firm hold on power. In the eighth and seventh centuries B.C., many Greeks established colonies in Asia Minor and along the coasts of the western Mediterranean. Greek colonists settled coastal towns in southern Italy and on the island of Sicily, an area that became known as Magna Graecia, meaning "Greater Greece."

In the mid-seventh century B.C., poor harvests and food shortages caused rioting in the Greek city-states. Individual rulers called "tyrants" overthrew many of the oligarchic governments. The tyrants seized property from landowning nobles and gave it to landless peasants and city dwellers. The tyrants also raised monuments and new buildings to glorify their reigns and to provide employment.

At the same time, national festivals, such as the Olympic Games, brought Greeks together to compete in athletic contests. Held every four years, these "Olympiads" halted all armed conflict among the Greeks. Other festivals took place in Corinth and in Delphi, the site of an important religious shrine.

THE RISE OF ATHENS

Many Greek rulers gradually extended citizenship (membership in their states) to artisans, merchants, and landowning peasants. Democracy—meaning "rule of the citizens"—replaced tyranny (rule by a tyrant) in several city-states. In Athens, a system of laws was developed by Cleisthenes, who overthrew the Athenian tyranny in 510 B.C. Cleisthenes established a ruling council of 500 members and extended voting rights to all adult men who were not slaves or prisoners.

Athens founded many colonies on the Aegean islands and became the wealthiest agricultural and commercial center of Greece. A large merchant navy carried on trade, provided defense, and brought back tribute from Athenian colonies. Within the city, a golden age of art, music, literature, and drama flowered in the fifth century B.C. Sculptors and architects beautified Athens with new temples, statues, buildings, and monuments.

Greek colonies on the coast of Asia Minor were also prospering and growing. Many of these settlements, however, had come under the control of the Persian Empire, a large and powerful Asian kingdom. After Athens supported a revolt against Persia in Asia Minor, the Persian king Darius I invaded Greece with a huge army. In 490 B.C., a small force of Athenian troops defeated the Persians at the Battle of Marathon. Ten years later, the Athenian navy repelled a second attack and drove the Persians back to Asia.

Statues of human figures, called caryatids, were designed to support the roof of a temple on the Acropolis of Athens. Damaged by the capital's severe pollution, the original caryatids were moved indoors to a museum and replaced by these replicas.

Athens and Sparta

After these military victories, Athens reached the height of its wealth and power.

Courtesy of Museo Nazionale, Naples

A brilliant tactical leader, Alexander the Great conquered the huge Persian Empire with a force of loyal Greek foot soldiers and cavalry. This mosaic depicts the Battle of Issus, where Alexander defeated the Persian king Darius III.

Under the leadership of Pericles, Athens formed a strong military alliance with other Greek city-states and colonies. To counter Athenian power, Sparta, a rival city-state, formed the Peloponnesian League with several of its allies. Although Athens controlled the region's most powerful navy, Spartan leaders commanded a large and disciplined land army.

In 431 B.C., the rivalry between Athens and Sparta erupted into the Peloponnesian War, a long conflict that brought widespread devastation and famine to cities, to rural areas, and to many islands. Sparta and its allies repeatedly attacked the countryside surrounding Athens, destroying the local harvests. In 429 B.C., Pericles, who had led the Athenian resistance to these raids, died during an outbreak of plague (a deadly disease) in Athens. With its economy shattered and its military might weakened, Athens finally accepted Sparta's terms for a truce in 404 B.C.

ALEXANDER THE GREAT

After the Peloponnesian War, the Greek city-states experienced further conflict and economic decline in the fourth century B.C. In northern Greece, however, the rising kingdom of Macedonia was gaining

new territory. Under the leadership of Philip II, Macedonia became the largest and strongest state of Greece. Philip planned to conquer the Persian Empire and prepared a large Greek army for an invasion. But an assassin murdered the Macedonian king before he could lead his forces into Asia.

Philip's son, known as Alexander the Great, succeeded him as king of Macedonia. Alexander first defeated several Greek states that opposed him. He then gathered a large army and swept through Asia Minor, Palestine (modern Israel), Egypt, and other lands controlled by the Persian Empire. The experienced Greek armies crushed the larger Persian forces by outmaneuvering them on the battlefield. After gaining their freedom from Persian domination, many cities and nations in Asia vowed their loyalty to Alexander's Macedonian Empire.

After defeating his opponents in the Middle East, Alexander pushed on to the mountains and deserts of central Asia and to the Indus River Valley in India. He established new cities and spread Greek science and philosophy to many of the peoples that had once opposed him. Greek became a commonly used language among

23

The Monument of Lysikrates, raised in 334 B.C., celebrated the victory of musicians and a chorus in a dramatic contest. Soon after the monument was completed, a burning tripod was placed on its top.

educated people in Asia and in lands along the coasts of the Mediterranean Sea. Several cities outside Greece, such as Alexandria in Egypt, became important centers of Greek culture.

Greece and Rome

After Alexander's death in 323 B.C., his generals divided the conquered territories among themselves. But without Alexander's leadership, the Macedonian Empire in Asia soon fell apart. In addition, during the third century B.C., several city-states joined forces to oppose Macedonian control of southern Greece. The continuing strife weakened Greece's defenses against outside invasion and caused an economic decline in many Greek cities.

At the same time, merchants from Rome, an expanding republic on the Italian Peninsula, were arriving in northwestern Greece. These traders were soon followed by Roman armies that seized large areas of the country. After launching a full-scale invasion of Greece and defeating the Macedonian army in 197 B.C., Rome established its rule over the Greek cities. By the first century B.C., Roman control had ended the frequent civil wars in Greece.

The Romans adopted the Greek religion and brought it to their cities and colonies throughout the Mediterranean. Despite the acceptance of Greek culture by the Romans, many Greeks protested foreign control, and a revolt erupted in 88 B.C. The Romans responded by attacking Athens and burning many Greek farms. After defeating another uprising in Corinth, the Romans made that city the capital of a new Roman province.

For two centuries after these rebellions, Greece remained peaceful. To defend the frontiers of their growing empire, the leaders of Rome sent their armies to other regions. But without these Roman defenses, the Greeks could not stop a devastating attack by Goths from northern Europe in A.D. 267. The Goths captured Athens and destroyed many other cities in central and southern Greece.

In the early fourth century, rivalries among Roman leaders and the continuing invasions from the north began to weaken the Roman Empire. At the same time, Christianity, a new religion that had originated in the Middle East, was gaining many supporters. In 330 the Roman emperor Constantine, who had converted to Christianity, moved the empire's capital

The Athenian tetradrachm coin was used throughout the Mediterranean region. On the coin is the head of Athena, the goddess who represented the city of Athens.

The Knights of St. John, a Christian brotherhood of the 1300s, built the Palace of the Grand Masters *(above)* **on the island of Rhodes. To protect themselves against attack, the group constructed a strong wall and a series of towers** *(below)* **around the city of Rhodes.**

from Rome to Byzantium. This Greek colony, which lay on the Bosporus Strait between Europe and Asia Minor, quickly grew in wealth and importance.

In 395 the Roman Empire was split into western and eastern realms. Rome remained the capital of the Western Empire. Constantinople (formerly Byzantium), a city with a large Greek population, became the capital of the Eastern (later called the Byzantine) Empire.

The Byzantine Empire

By the early sixth century, the Byzantine Empire had achieved prosperity and stability. In addition to Greece, the realm included other territories in the Balkan Peninsula, Asia Minor, the Middle East, and North Africa. Although the Byzantine legal system was Roman, the official language of the empire was Greek.

The emperor Justinian, who ruled from 527 to 565, enlarged the empire through further conquests in Africa, Italy, and Spain. Byzantine missionaries spread the Christian faith to cities in Asia as well as to Slavic peoples who had settled southeastern Europe. Justinian's campaigns, however, drained the empire's finances. Maintaining armies to defend Greece and other territories in the far-flung empire became difficult. After the death of Justinian, waves of Slavic armies from eastern Europe overran much of Greece.

For several centuries after the arrival of the Slavs, Greece suffered frequent attacks by other European peoples. Armed bands of Vikings from Sweden and Norway raided the Greek coasts. Normans and Franks from western Europe seized harbor towns and many Aegean islands. The Norman and Frankish armies were led by dukes who established personal domains in the larger Greek cities such as Athens and Thessaloniki.

Despite the loss of much of its Greek territory, the Byzantine Empire remained strong and prosperous. In the ninth century, Basil I became the first member of a new dynasty (family of rulers) from Macedonia. During the next 200 years, the Macedonian emperors recaptured territory in northern Greece, restored trade, and built many new churches and monasteries.

RELIGIOUS DISPUTES AND DIVISION

In 1054 a dispute between religious leaders in Rome and Constantinople led to the division of the Christian church into rival Latin (Roman Catholic) and Greek (Eastern Orthodox) factions. Constantinople became the center of the new Eastern Orthodox Church, which conducted its rituals in Greek. The Greeks followed the teachings of Eastern Orthodox clergy.

After this religious division, the military ties between Byzantine leaders and the Catholic pope in Rome weakened. Normans from Europe and Saracens from North Africa continued to invade Byzantine territory. Among the invaders were Roman Catholic crusaders who were traveling through the empire to fight religious wars in the Middle East. In 1204 crusaders from France and from Venice, a wealthy Italian city, captured and sacked Constantinople. Rulers loyal to the Latin church replaced the Macedonian dynasty in Constantinople, establishing the Latin Empire.

During the thirteenth century, Venetians took control of Crete and of several Ionian Islands. Noble families from several states

Osios Loukas, an Eastern Orthodox monastery, was dedicated to a hermit who fled to a nearby village from invading Saracens in the tenth century. Monasteries became important refuges during the Middle Ages (fifth to the fourteenth centuries), a time of frequent unrest and invasion throughout Greece.

Photo by Drs. A. A. M. van der Heyden, Naarden, the Netherlands

Michael Paleologus led the fight to depose the Latin rulers of the Byzantine Empire and to replace them with Greeks.

in western Europe set up semi-independent realms on the Greek mainland. The Frenchman Geoffrey de Villehardouin built new castles, cities, and Latin churches in his domain on the Peloponnesus. These small states did not coordinate their military forces, however. In 1261 the general Michael Paleologus rallied a large army of Greek soldiers. Paleologus overcame the defenses of the Latin Empire and recaptured Constantinople.

The Ottoman Conquest

Although Paleologus restored the Byzantine Empire, it now covered a much smaller area. In the 1300s, most of Greece remained a patchwork of small domains ruled by foreigners. For example, the island of Euboea was still in Venetian hands, and Rhodes belonged to a group of Christian knights who had fought in the Crusades. Without central control, much

The capture of Constantinople by the Ottoman Turks in 1453 ended the Byzantine Empire, which had governed parts of Greece for nearly a thousand years. After the conquest of Constantinople – which they renamed Istanbul – Ottoman leaders established a vast empire of their own in eastern Europe, the Middle East, and North Africa.

of the countryside remained vulnerable to foreign invasion.

The unsuccessful efforts of Byzantine rulers to recapture Greek lands, as well as unrest in many Byzantine cities, weakened the empire. In addition, invaders from Asia—the Ottoman Turks—had conquered Asia Minor and were threatening Constantinople. Macedonia fell to the Turks in 1371, and Constantinople barely escaped a Turkish attack in 1397.

The Turks, who followed the Islamic religion, returned with a larger force in 1453 and captured Constantinople. By 1460 the Turks had driven the Venetians and other western Europeans from southern Greece, although Venice kept control of the Ionian Islands. Gradually, the Ottoman Empire absorbed the rest of the Byzantine realm. The Turkish sultan (king) ruled this territory from Constantinople, which the Turks renamed Istanbul.

Turkish commanders kept firm control of Greek cities, ports, and islands for several centuries after the fall of Constantinople. The Turks ruled through pashas—leaders with complete authority over their provinces. The pashas employed local officials to collect taxes, to run the courts, and to administer the cities.

After Turkish troops put down uprisings in the fifteenth and sixteenth centuries, many Greeks fled the country. The Turks allowed the Greeks who remained some economic independence, however, and the Eastern Orthodox Church survived. But for several centuries Greece was cut off from the scientific and economic advances taking place in other parts of Europe. Athens, once wealthy and powerful, became a poor farming village. The Turkish rulers, who used the country as a source of money and soldiers, gained income from Greek trade and agriculture.

The War for Independence

In the late 1700s, the Greeks began a strong drive for independence from Turkish rule. The movement gained much of its support from successful Greek merchants and traders who operated new factories and a large shipping fleet. Russia, an eastern European empire that opposed Turkish control of the Balkan Peninsula, encouraged the Greek nationalists to revolt. Britain and France, western European countries, also assisted the Greek independence movement. These powers sought to resist Turkish expansion into the Mediterranean and to protect their political and commercial ties in the region. Under the terms of a European peace treaty of 1815, Britain established control over the Ionian Islands, which had experienced a short period of independence from Venice after 1797.

In 1821 an armed force under Alexander Ypsilanti entered the Balkan Peninsula and proclaimed the independence of Greece.

Independent Picture Service

The exploits of Theodore Kolokotronis (1770–1843), a general in the Greek War of Independence, have become the subject of many Greek folk songs.

Modern Greece came into being over a period of 120 years after the end of the Greek War of Independence. Greek-speaking regions belonging to the Ottoman Empire, to Britain, and to Italy were added to Greece during the nineteenth and early twentieth centuries. The last region to become formally Greek was the Dodecanese Islands, a group which Italy ceded to Greece after World War II.

Artwork by Laura Westlund

Independent Picture Service

On March 25, 1821, at Kalavrita in the northern Peloponnesus, Archbishop Germanos of Patras proclaimed the start of the Greek struggle for independence.

Although the Turks eventually defeated Ypsilanti, violent uprisings occurred in many regions of the occupied country. The Turks were soon forced to withdraw from central Greece and from some Aegean islands. Egypt helped the Turks by invading the Peloponnesus in 1825. But in 1827 a fleet of French, British, and Russian ships defeated the Turkish and Egyptian navies at the Battle of Navarino. After this defeat off the coast of the Peloponnesus, Turkish forces abandoned southern Greece.

A newly established Greek national assembly then drew up a constitution and named Count Ioannis Kapodistrias, a Russian-trained Greek diplomat, as the first president of the Republic of Greece. The leaders of the Ottoman Empire agreed to peace terms in 1829. At the same time, France, Britain, and Russia pledged to protect Greek independence.

Independent Picture Service

Ioannis Kapodistrias, who became the first president of the Republic of Greece in 1827, is commemorated in numerous modern monuments. The stern Kapodistrias was assassinated in 1831 while still in office.

The Greek Kingdom

The new Greek state consisted of the Peloponnesus, the Cyclades Islands, and central Greece. The Ottoman Empire maintained control over northern Greece, Crete, and islands in the eastern Aegean. Many Greeks were dissatisfied with these boundaries and sought to bring all of the Greek-speaking areas in the region into the new nation. In addition, Kapodistrias's stern rule caused unrest and growing opposition to the republic's central government. After Kapodistrias was assassinated in 1831, civil war broke out between opposing Greek factions.

In an attempt to settle the political turmoil, the European powers created a kingdom in Greece and offered the throne to a German prince—Otto of Bavaria. Otto, who was only 17 when he became King Otto I in 1833, depended on advisers to help him rule the country. These foreign officials imposed heavy taxes and denied the Greeks a new constitution.

To support Otto, the European powers continued to play an important role in the country's defense and government. Foreign rule angered many Greeks, however, and economic difficulties weakened Otto's authority. In 1843, while the king was traveling abroad, Greek nationalists forced Otto's advisers to flee the country. When he returned, Otto had no choice but to accept a new constitution that diminished his role in the government.

Throughout the 1840s and 1850s, Greece continued to experience unrest and financial problems. In 1862 the Greek army revolted against Otto, who was forced to give up his throne. The British nominated the Danish prince William George as the new monarch. The Greeks agreed to crown the prince as King George I of the Hellenes in 1863. To reward the Greeks for their acceptance of the new king, Britain returned the Ionian Islands. A new constitution in 1864 further limited the king's powers and granted voting rights to Greek men. The constitution also established a unicameral (one-house) parliament.

Photo by Bettmann Archive

Only 17 when he became king of Greece, Otto I of Bavaria ruled the kingdom with the help of many advisers and with the support of foreign powers.

FURTHER CONFLICT WITH THE TURKS

Greece continued to demand the return of territory still under Turkish control, finally declaring war in 1878. The European powers stopped the fighting and asked Turkey to give up Thessaly and Epirus. The Turks ceded Thessaly to Greece in 1881 but maintained control of western Epirus.

When an uprising against Turkish rule erupted on the island of Crete in 1896, Greek forces attacked the Turks in Macedonia. Turkey declared war and defeated Greece in a few weeks. But in 1898 the European powers, which had again arranged for a truce, set up an independent government for Crete. Prince George, the son of King George I of Britain, became the island's high commissioner.

The Cretans, led by Eleutherios Venizelos, resisted Prince George's leadership and demanded union with the rest of Greece. Guerrilla bands formed in the island's many isolated and mountainous regions. Threatened with a violent uprising, Prince George resigned, and the European powers withdrew their forces from the island. Although Crete was not recognized internationally as part of Greece, the Cretan legislature proclaimed the union in 1908.

In 1910 Venizelos became the prime minister of the Kingdom of Greece. Although he faced opposition from the Greek army, Venizelos enacted many economic and educational reforms. Under his leadership, Greece built new roads, railroads, and modern industries.

Under Eleutherios Venizelos, who became prime minister of Greece in 1910, new roads and industries were built in the country. Crete and other regions also became united with the republic. Venizelos, however, fought with the Greek military and with royalist supporters of the Greek monarchy, and was forced into exile in 1935.

Photo by Bettmann Archive

Turkish troops storm a village during the conflict between Greeks and Turks that flared after World War I. Although Greeks had lived in Asia Minor (modern Turkey) since ancient times, the defeat of Greek forces in the early 1920s led to a mass emigration of ethnic Greeks from Turkey. The arrival of these refugees in Greece caused widespread unemployment during the 1920s and early 1930s.

Greek unrest in Turkish-held lands continued, especially in Macedonia, a region where both Greeks and Bulgarians were demanding independence. In 1912 Greece allied with several Balkan countries to defeat the Turks, who were forced to return Macedonia to Greece. But Bulgarian demands for more territory in Macedonia led to a second Balkan war, which pitted Greece against Bulgaria. As a result of the conflict, Greece lost part of Macedonia but gained western Epirus, several Aegean islands, and part of Thrace. Crete also became officially united with Greece.

World War I and the Postwar Crisis

Despite these victories, divisions within the Greek government persisted, and this conflict worsened when World War I broke out in 1914. Britain, France, and their allies fought the war against Germany and Turkey. Constantine I—who had succeeded his father, King George, in 1913—supported Germany. Venizelos resigned from the government in 1915 and backed Britain and France. In 1916 Venizelos and his supporters established a new government in Thessaloniki to oppose Constantine. In the next year, Constantine gave up his throne in favor of his son, George II. Greece then entered the war on the side of the Allies.

World War I ended with the defeat of Germany and Turkey in 1918. Under a treaty signed in 1920, Greece received more territory in Thrace, several more Aegean islands, and the city of Smyrna in western Turkey. The Turks, however, were determined to fight for Smyrna. Clashes broke out in Asia Minor, and by 1922 the defeated Greek armies were fleeing. A treaty returned the city to Turkey, forcing more than a million Greek residents of Smyrna and the surrounding region to resettle in Greece.

The defeat at Smyrna and a severe economic depression brought instability to the Greek kingdom. Both Venizelos and Constantine I—who had returned to the throne in 1920—lost support. In 1924 the Greek parliament proclaimed Greece a republic. The nation's government became divided between republicans, who supported a representative assembly, and royalists, who backed the return of a strong monarchy.

In the late 1920s, a series of military leaders took power in Greece. None of them, however, could solve the country's many financial problems. The worldwide economic depression of the early 1930s—as well as the large number of refugees who had entered Greece from Turkey in the 1920s—caused severe unemployment and widespread poverty.

After royalist representatives won the legislative elections of 1935, a popular vote returned George II, Constantine's son, to the restored throne of Greece. The opposing factions held nearly equal numbers of seats in the Greek parliament, giving the small Greek Communist party the deciding vote on many important issues. As a result, Greek leaders were unable to govern the country effectively.

The Greek military saw the continuing legislative deadlock and widespread unrest among urban workers as threats to the country's security. In 1936 General Ioannis Metaxas, with the support of the king, led a military takeover, dissolving the legislature and banning political parties.

World War II

In the 1930s, while Greece was facing economic decline and political turmoil, Germany and Italy were establishing a strong military alliance. After Germany attacked Poland in September 1939, Britain and France declared war on Germany. These events resulted in the outbreak of World War II.

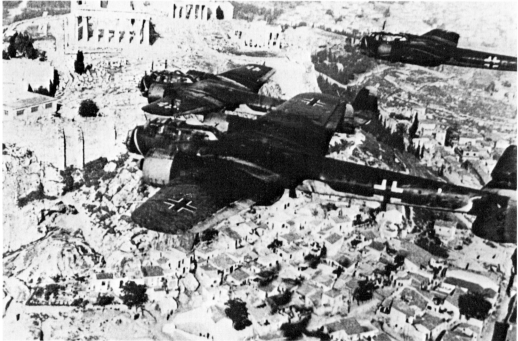

Photo by Ullstein Bilderdienst

German bombers fly over Athens during the attack on Greece in April 1941. The powerful planes, tanks, and artillery of the German forces overwhelmed Greek opposition in a few weeks, leading to a three-year occupation of the country.

A massive rally in Athens in 1946 occurred after the first free Greek elections in 10 years. Many Greeks believed that the elections, which brought a royalist government to power, had been unfair. Protests such as this one worsened a violent conflict between Communist and royalist forces which continued until 1949.

Although Greece did not take sides in the conflict, Italian troops attacked northern Greece after invading Albania in 1940. The Greek forces put up a strong resistance, provoking Germany to invade the country in April 1941. On April 23, the Greek government signed a truce, and German armies began a long occupation. After fleeing Greece, King George established a government-in-exile in London.

Greeks formed several resistance bands to oppose the Germans. Although they fought for a common goal, these groups were split by their political beliefs. The largest such group favored a Communist-style government that would abolish private property and give political power to workers and farmers. Another resistance group was made up of royalists and others who opposed the Communists. As the war progressed, conflict often broke out between these organizations.

CIVIL WAR AND RECOVERY

By the summer of 1944, German armies were retreating in western Europe and from the Balkan Peninsula. After the Germans withdrew from Greece in the fall, the exiled Greek government returned to Athens. Communist guerrillas, however, controlled much of rural Greece and fought with police and army units in the Greek capital. In December civil war broke out between government forces and guerrilla soldiers in rural Greece. The conflict caused widespread destruction and famine until 1949, when the poorly armed Communists agreed to a truce.

In the 1950s, Greece began a slow recovery from the damages of the civil war. In 1952 the country joined the North Atlantic Treaty Organization (NATO), a military alliance of the United States and several western European nations. Greek women won the right to vote and to run

Greece adopted its flag after gaining independence in the nineteenth century. The cross in the upper left corner of the flag stands for the country's religious traditions. The flag's nine stripes represent the nine syllables of the Greek words *eleutheria a thanatos* (meaning "liberty or death").

Artwork by Laura Westlund

for election to the legislature. Constantine Karamanlis, a conservative politician who desired closer economic cooperation with western Europe, became prime minister in 1956. With extensive U.S. aid, Greek industry and agriculture expanded throughout the 1950s. Karamanlis's administration also kept wages and prices under control.

Political Turmoil and Dictatorship

Despite the improving economy, political rivalries continued to divide the country in the 1960s. A new party—formed by Georgios Papandreou—opposed Karamanlis, who resigned his position in 1963. Papandreou then succeeded Karamanlis as prime minister.

After speaking out against a strong monarchy, Papandreou came under attack by members of the armed forces and by Constantine II, who had become king in 1964. After the king fired Papandreou in 1965, several Greek governments rose and fell during a series of bitter disputes. As in the 1930s, Greek army officers felt that political rivalries and instability were hurting the country.

In April 1967, a group of army colonels overthrew the government, arresting many politicians and setting up a military junta (ruling committee). The junta, led by Colonel Georgios Papadopoulos, imposed strict censorship on the press and outlawed political activity. King Constantine went into exile after trying and failing to overthrow Papadopoulos. In 1968 the junta drew up a new constitution that banned all elections.

Despite these harsh measures, the junta released many political prisoners and restored some civil rights in the early 1970s. In 1973 the junta abolished the monarchy and proclaimed Greece a republic, with Papadopoulos as president. When violent antigovernment demonstrations broke out later in the year, the junta imposed martial law (rule by military decree).

Papadopoulos was unable to restore order, and a group of officers deposed him in November. Despite the change in leadership, the military junta continued to impose censorship and resumed imprisoning political opponents.

Under military rule, Greece suffered increasing isolation from western Europe. The junta's leaders were not trained for diplomacy or for guiding the Greek economy. In 1974 Greek officers helped to overthrow the leader of Cyprus, an island state in the eastern Mediterranean. Both Greeks and Turks lived on Cyprus, which had won its independence from British rule in 1960. After the Greeks deposed the island's leader, Turkish forces invaded northern Cyprus. The two sides soon agreed to a cease-fire, and the island was divided into northern (Turkish-speaking) and southern (Greek-speaking) zones. In Greece, the conflict was seen as a defeat and a scandal. In July 1974, the junta resigned, and Constantine Karamanlis returned to head a civilian government.

RETURN TO DEMOCRACY

Two new political parties formed after the fall of the junta. The socialist party PASOK, headed by Andreas Papandreou, favored government control of major industries. The conservative New Democracy party supported a limited role for government in the economy. Karamanlis, who became head of the New Democracy party, won election as prime minister in 1974. In addition, Greek voters rejected the return of the Greek monarchy. In 1975 a new constitution was approved that established a president as head of state and a prime minister to run the government.

After writing the new constitution, the Greek government turned its attention to the troubled economy. To improve trade, Karamanlis sought to take advantage of the large market for goods in western Europe. In 1981 Greece became a member of the European Community (EC), an economic alliance of western European nations. Later that year, PASOK won a majority in parliament, and Andreas Papandreou became the country's first socialist prime minister.

Recent Events

During the 1980s, the dispute between Greece and Turkey over Cyprus continued

to dominate Greece's foreign policy. In 1983 Turkish Cypriot leaders established the Republic of Northern Cyprus, a state that has not gained recognition outside of Turkey. The Greek and Turkish governments have been unable to agree on the island's future status.

In the early 1990s, the breakup of Yugoslavia led to war in the Balkan Peninsula. Macedonia, the Yugoslav republic that lay on Greece's northern border, declared its independence as the Republic of Macedonia. Angered by the use of the name "Macedonia," which the Greek government feels should only refer to the northern region of Greece, Greek officials banned trade to Macedonia through Thessaloniki. In 1995 the two nations agreed to resume trade and to negotiate on the future name of the new republic.

The New Democracy party defeated PASOK by a slight majority in the 1990 elections. Constantine Mitsotakis, the successor to Karamanlis as head of the party, became prime minister. But in 1993, Mitsotakis resigned his post after the New Democracy party lost its majority in Parliament. The resignation forced a special

Artwork by Laura Westlund

The official state arms of Greece feature the white-on-blue cross also seen on the Greek flag.

election in the fall of that year.

The victory of PASOK in the election then turned Andreas Papandreou as prime minister. But failing health prevented Papandreou from leading the government. Opposed by several members of his cabinet, Papandreou resigned in early 1996. The new PASOK leader, Konstantinos Simitis, replaced Papandreou, who died that spring.

Government

The government of the Republic of Greece is based on the 1975 constitution, which established a presidency and a one-house parliament. All Greek citizens 18 years of age or older may vote for members of the Greek parliament, who serve four-year terms. Members of parliament, in turn, elect the president, who serves a five-year term as head of state.

The prime minister, who is usually the head of the party holding the most seats in parliament, names the cabinet of ministers. Although the prime minister controls the day-to-day operations of the government, the president has a limited right to dissolve parliament. The president must consult the Council of the Republic, a committee of Greek political leaders, on important decisions affecting the legislature and constitution.

Within the Greek judicial system, lower courts hear criminal cases. Appeals of lower-court decisions can be made to a court of appeals or to the Greek Supreme Court. A constitutional court rules on cases affecting parliament and the constitution.

Greece consists of 13 regions and 51 departments (or *nomoi*). A *nomarch*, appointed by the minister of the interior, governs each department. A city council and a mayor administer cities of more than 100,000 residents. Smaller towns elect presidents and community councils.

Photo by Bettmann Archive

Constantine Mitsotakis, leader of the conservative New Democracy party, celebrated his organization's victory in local elections during 1986. Mitsotakis became the Greek prime minister after New Democracy won national elections in 1990.

Townspeople crowd outdoor cafes and sidewalks on the island of Hydra. A stroll in the early evening is traditional among Greeks, whether they live in large cities, small towns, or island villages.

3) The People

About 72 percent of Greece's 10.5 million people live in urban areas. Since the late 1940s, Greek cities have grown rapidly as many rural and island people have arrived in search of manufacturing jobs. Although the population density of Greece is high, much of the countryside is made up of sparsely inhabited highlands.

Since ancient times, Greeks have faced a shortage of natural resources and of fertile soil. These conditions led to emigration and to the colonization of foreign lands. In the twentieth century, famine and economic depression spurred many Greeks to seek better opportunities in western Europe, North America, and Australia.

Ethnic Identity and Language

About 94 percent of the people of Greece are Greek speaking and of Greek heritage. The long period of Turkish rule, as well as invasion by various European powers, brought about a greater ethnic mixture in Attica, in the Peloponnesus, and on the Aegean islands. Many Greeks living in remote regions, such as Epirus, are direct descendants of the country's first settlers from northern and eastern Europe.

Greece is also home to several minority groups. Turkish-speakers, most of whom live in Thrace and on the Dodecanese Islands, make up about 4 percent of the population. In the early 1990s, many Albanian emigrants fled to northern Epirus to escape political unrest in their country. Bulgarian and other Balkan peoples also inhabit Greece's northern regions.

An ancient Indo-European tongue, Greek is the everyday language of nearly all Greek citizens. In the northwestern region of Thrace and on the Dodecanese Islands, ethnic Turks use Turkish as their first language. Slavic tongues are common in

This street vendor in Athens sells thick pretzel rolls, a popular snack throughout Greece. On the pole are national lottery tickets, which Greeks can also buy from small stores and from official lottery agencies.

northern areas that border Greece's Balkan neighbors.

The Greek alphabet, which has 24 letters, became the basis for the Latin and Cyrillic alphabets used in western European and Slavic languages, respectively. Modern spoken Greek, also known as demotic Greek, contains words and phrases borrowed from Turkish and Italian. Although many demotic words are similar to the words of ancient Greek, modern Greeks need study and practice to read and understand the works of ancient writers.

Costumed Greek dancers do a traditional line dance. Folk dances are still known to nearly all Greeks and are performed in village squares, city taverns, and schools.

Ancient artisans carved this inscription in stone that excavators found at the ancient site of Delphi. Wealthy Greeks often used these stones to record dedications of religious temples and public donations to the Greek gods.

Two special forms of Greek—*koine* and *katharevousa*—are still in use. During religious services, clergy of the Greek Orthodox Church use koine Greek, the original language of the Bible's New Testament. The eighteenth-century inventor of katharevousa, Adamantios Korais, tried to improve demotic Greek by introducing words and grammar from ancient Greek. Katharevousa has remained the official language of government, of scholarly writing, and of some newspapers. Over the years, however, demotic Greek has replaced katharevousa in most of the country's newspapers and magazines.

Health and Education

Health care in Greece is most readily available in the larger cities. Many people living in small villages or in rural areas must travel long distances to find hospitals or adequate medical care. The government maintains social-security programs for the country's workers and provides pensions and medical benefits to retired people.

Compared to most European countries, Greece has a low birthrate (10 births per 1,000 people). The rate of infant mortality —the number of babies who die within one year of birth—is 8.3 per 1,000 live births. This figure is also lower than average for

Greek monks decorated this religious text with ink, paints, and paper-thin sheets of gold leaf. The manuscript was written in *koine* Greek during the reign of the Byzantine emperors.

41

Young Greeks exercise during a school recess. Many elementary students wear uniforms in blue and white, the colors of the Greek flag.

Europe. Life expectancy in Greece, at 77 years, is comparable to average lifespans in the rest of Europe.

Greek law requires children to attend school from the ages of 6 to 15, but many students continue their studies until age 18. Students begin with a six-year elementary curriculum and then attend two secondary-school courses that last for three years each. The gymnasium, for seventh through ninth grades, instructs students in history, literature, geography, and other basic subjects. Students must pass entrance examinations to enter the lyceum, a school for the tenth through twelfth grades. One kind of lyceum covers general academic fields and the other has a technical and vocational curriculum.

A shortage of schools and teachers exists in some rural areas of the country. Although all Greek towns have primary schools, some areas lack secondary schools. The government has funded extensive literacy programs, and the percentage of adults who can read has risen from 60 percent in the early twentieth century to more than 90 percent in the early 1990s.

Sixteen universities, including the University of Athens, operate in Greece. Other postsecondary institutions in the capital include schools of archaeology, business, and the arts. The National Polytechnic University instructs the country's future engineers and scientists. Foreign countries have established schools of archaeology and literature in Athens.

Literature

The earliest Greek literature was epic poetry performed by wandering bards (singing poets). Scholars believe that one such poet, Homer, wrote *The Iliad*, a long narrative epic about a war between the Greeks of Mycenae and the armies of Troy, a city in Asia Minor. *The Odyssey*, also attributed to Homer, follows the voyages of the hero Odysseus in the Mediterranean world. Written nearly 3,000 years ago, these epics depict traditional Greek heroes, gods, and goddesses. Popular among both ancient and modern Greeks, *The Iliad* and *The Odyssey* have remained the most famous works of Greek literature.

Hesiod, who lived during the seventh century B.C., honored the rural way of life in *Works and Days*, a collection of his verse. Sappho, a woman from the island of Lesbos, became the most famous writer of Greek love poems. Other poetry, such as the odes of Pindar, honored athletic heroes.

Drama developed as ancient Greek writers combined music and poetry for public performance in outdoor theaters. Aeschylus, Sophocles, and Euripides based their tragedies on Greek legends. Aristophanes wrote comedies that made fun of the well-known political and literary figures of his time.

The ancient Greeks also pioneered the writing of history and biography. Herodotus traveled widely in Asia, Africa, and southern Europe. His accounts of foreign peoples and religions fascinated the Greeks of the fifth century B.C. Thucydides' history of the Peloponnesian War relied on firsthand accounts of soldiers who fought in the conflict. Plutarch, who was born in Greece during its rule by the Romans, wrote about the lives of well-known Romans and Greeks.

Greek philosophy began in the teachings of famous thinkers who organized schools in Athens and other cities. During the fifth century B.C., the philosopher Socrates held informal discussions among Athenians on

Independent Picture Service

Euripides (480–406 B.C.), considered one of the greatest ancient Greek playwrights, introduced realistic situations into classic Greek myths.

Independent Picture Service

Odysseus Elytis, a Nobel Prize-winning poet, is best known for *The Axion Esti*. The autobiographical poem takes its title, which means "worthy it is," from the first line of a religious hymn.

politics, religion, and the law. Many of these dialogues were written down by his student Plato, who set forth his own ideal of good government in *The Republic*. Aristotle, a teacher of Alexander the Great, wrote volumes on science, law, ethics, and literature. Aristotle's works influenced philosophy and science in western Europe long after his death in 322 B.C.

From the fifth to the fifteenth centuries A.D., Greek writers of the Byzantine Empire turned to religious poetry and to interpreting Christian doctrine. After the fall of the empire in 1453, a tradition of folktales and poetry continued within Turkish-occupied Greece. Stories and poems in demotic Greek flourished after Greece became independent in the 1820s.

The New School of Athens, a group of writers and poets, brought new vitality to Greek writing in the early twentieth century. Constantine Kavafis—a Greek poet who lived in Alexandria, Egypt—wrote expressive verse about the ancient Greeks and Romans. The most famous modern Greek author, Nikos Kazantzakis, was a Cretan whose works have been translated into many languages. His novels, including *Zorba the Greek,* describe the struggle of the individual for knowledge and freedom. In 1963 the poet George Seferis became the first Greek to win the Nobel Prize for literature. Odysseus Elytis, a painter and poet from Crete, won the prize in 1979.

Visual Arts

Archaeologists have unearthed sculpture and pottery from the earliest civilizations of southern Greece and the Aegean islands. Most of these works depict ancient Greek deities. The *kouros,* or figure of a young boy, and the *kore,* or figure of a young girl, were common statues in the homes and public buildings of ancient Greece. By the fifth century B.C., Greek artists were carving statues of politicians, athletes, and

The knights who built the Palace of the Grand Masters in Rhodes commissioned numerous artworks, including this mosaic. Made up of colored stones joined together on floors or wall panels, mosaics were a common household decoration for wealthy citizens of ancient Greece and of the Byzantine Empire.

View of Toledo, the most famous work of Domenikos Theotokopoulos, depicts an old Spanish city in a striking arrangement of light, clouds, and landscape. Also known as El Greco (meaning "the Greek" in Spanish), Theotokopoulos was born on Crete but spent most of his adult life in Spain.

mythological figures. Two of the finest Athenian sculptors, Phidias and Praxiteles, created works for marketplaces, temples, and the homes of wealthy citizens.

Although the ancient Greeks painted sculptures and the walls of temples and homes, few of their paintings have survived. Lively wall murals found in Minoan buildings on Crete and Santorini show religious processions, athletic contests, and sea voyages. Scenes of Homeric legends and of everyday life decorate pottery used in trade and as household utensils.

During the golden age of Athens in the fifth century B.C., professional architects designed public buildings known as *stoas,* as well as open-air theaters that included sculpted figures and backdrops. The Acropolis, a hilltop stronghold in Athens, contains the remains of the Parthenon, a magnificent temple. Built and decorated by the skilled architects and sculptors of Athens, the Parthenon became an important symbol of ancient Greece.

After the rise of Christianity in Greece, icons—or decorated wooden panels—were a popular form of religious painting. Artists also ornamented church walls and domes with religious mosaics made up of small colored stones. Domenikos Theotokopoulos (1541–1614), also known as El Greco, was a painter from Crete who lived and worked in Spain. His portraits and landscapes are famous for their dramatic colors and for the artist's startling use of light and shade.

Religion and Festivals

More than 95 percent of Greeks belong to the Greek Orthodox Church, a branch of the Eastern Orthodox Church. Divided from the Roman Catholic Church in the eleventh century, the Orthodox church was

Courtesy of Gretchen Bratvold

Greek (Eastern) Orthodox priests preside at services, weddings, baptisms, and funerals. Church officials also participate in various religious celebrations that are observed by feasting and processions in Greek towns and villages.

tant churches. During World War II, the German occupation forces sent many Jews, who once made up a large percentage of the population of Thessaloniki, to concentration camps in eastern Europe. A small number of Jews, most of whom now live in Athens, remain in Greece.

Easter is the most important religious holiday for Orthodox Greeks. During the week before Easter, fireworks and feasting accompany religious processions and services in many Greek towns. Each village honors its patron saint on the saint's feast day. Although Greeks also celebrate Christmas, they exchange gifts on St. Basil's Day—January 1.

March 25, Greek Independence Day, marks the Greek revolt against Turkish occupation that began in 1821. Ochi (meaning "no") Day on October 28 is another patriotic holiday. On this day, Greeks celebrate the refusal of General Metaxas to meet Italian demands during World War II.

an important part of Greek life during centuries of foreign occupation. Many Greek emigrants remain active church members in their adopted homelands.

The Greek government financially supports the Orthodox church, and religion is taught in the country's public schools. In 1982, however, the government legalized civil marriage and relaxed its strict laws concerning divorce. The Orthodox church is now less important in the everyday lives of most Greeks than it was during the Turkish occupation. Church attendance has declined but remains high on religious holidays and for baptisms, weddings, and funerals.

Most Turks living within Greece practice the Islamic religion. A minority of Greeks belong to the Roman Catholic and Protes-

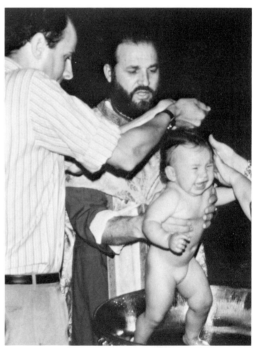

Photo by Ioannis Epaminondas

Baptism into the Greek Orthodox faith is a rite common to many Greek-speakers throughout the world.

During a festival in a small Greek town, people roast whole lambs over an open charcoal pit.

Food

Greeks eat small meals during the day and reserve substantial fare for the late evening. At the evening meal, a first course of *mezedhes,* or appetizers, may consist of tomatoes, cucumbers, olives, peppers, and a goat cheese called feta. Popular main dishes include souvlaki—grilled meat served on skewers—and *loukanika* (spiced sausages). *Dolmades* are rolled grape leaves stuffed with meat and rice. Moussaka and *pastitio* are mixtures of meat and vegetables served as a casserole. Greeks also enjoy a wide variety of seafood, including octopus, lobster, shrimp, squid, and mullet.

Music and dancing often accompany dinner in Greek *tavernas,* many of which stay open into the morning hours. The tavernas prepare generous portions of traditional Greek food and serve Greek wines, such as *retsina,* straight from huge barrels.

Sweet desserts traditionally follow Greek meals. Baklava and *kataifi* combine pastry and honey. Also popular are yogurt, custard, and fresh fruit. Greeks drink thick, strong coffee at home, in cafes, and in offices throughout the day. Vineyards in southern Greece produce both red and white wines, as well as *retsina* (wine flavored with pine resin). Some adults enjoy ouzo, a strong liqueur, before dinner.

Sports and Recreation

Many Greeks take a keen interest in competitive sports, and some participate as members of organized clubs. The country's most popular group sport is soccer. Greek soccer leagues include teams from all large towns and cities. Greece has also sent national teams to European and international soccer championships. Professional and amateur athletes play basketball, another

Photo by Robert L. Wolfe

Greeks love sweet desserts such as *melopita* (left), which is a honey-and-cheese pie, and orange yogurt cake (right). Thick, sweet coffee is often served with these desserts after a heavy meal.

Thousands of miles of beaches line the mainland and islands of Greece. The warm waters and sandy shores attract millions of tourists during the winter months.

popular spectator sport. The Greek national basketball team recently won the European championship.

Greece, the home of the ancient Olympic Games, was also the site of the first modern Olympics in 1896. In that year, Spiridon Louis, a Greek water carrier, won the first Olympic marathon. Many other athletic contests, including wrestling and discus throwing, originated in ancient Greece. The country's public schools maintain programs in most track-and-field events.

Water sports—such as sailing, water-skiing, windsurfing, and scuba diving—are popular in Greece's coastal waters. Snow-skiing trails have been built in Epirus and on the slopes of Mount Parnassus in central Greece. The rugged Greek highlands also offer opportunities for hiking and mountain climbing.

This painting on an ancient jar depicts Olympic athletes running a footrace. The original Olympic Games also included discus and javelin throwing, wrestling, and boxing.

49

Oil discoveries off the coast of Thasos provide a small portion of Greece's needed energy supplies. Despite these recent finds, Greece still imports most of its oil.

4) The Economy

In the 1950s and 1960s, the Greek economy slowly recovered from the damages caused by World War II. The government supported new industries and encouraged foreign investment. But developers built most new factories near Athens, forcing the rest of the country to rely on farming and other traditional industries. A lack of planning and coordination also slowed economic growth.

By the 1980s, inflation and unemployment were serious problems. The Greek government was also running large budget deficits. Inefficient management of state-owned industries was an important cause of the deficits, which hurt new investment. Attempts to privatize (sell off) state-owned industries, such as the telecommunications system, have brought strong opposition from workers who fear losing their jobs.

After Greece joined the European Union, trade with western Europe increased. But EU membership has brought a serious dilemma in the 1990s. As the EU plans to create a single European currency, Greece and other members must reach certain economic targets, including lower inflation, rising productivity, and smaller budget deficits. The strict budgets planned by the PASOK government to reach these goals have helped to lower inflation. But cuts in social services and benefits have angered many Greek citizens, leading to strikes and political turmoil.

Manufacturing

Manufacturing in Greece expanded rapidly during the 1970s, becoming the most important sector of the nation's economy. Some heavy industries still use outdated equipment and methods, and many smaller Greek businesses are run inefficiently. The country has also been slow to invest in modern equipment such as industrial robots, although computers are now common in many Greek companies.

Greek firms have built several new industrial complexes in cooperation with foreign investors. For example, French companies helped to construct and operate a large aluminum plant. A Greek-U.S. partnership financed a refinery complex near Thessaloniki that processes crude oil, manufactures steel, and produces petroleum-based goods, such as plastics and fertilizers.

Factories that process food, beverages, and tobacco still make up the largest industry in Greece. Many of these companies are small operations that need only seasonal workers. Although competition

For many years, Greek factories suffered from outdated facilities and low productivity. Since the early 1970s, however, new investment in manufacturing facilities has brought modern equipment and methods to plants, such as this one near Athens.

Courtesy of OPIC

51

In Greece, laborers harvest olives by beating the tree branches with long poles and then collecting the fruit that falls to the ground.

pand. Greek companies have also raised new homes in the Middle East and in Africa.

Greece's extensive port facilities support busy ship-repair and shipbuilding industries. Shipyards near Athens and on the island of Syros manufacture ferries, fishing boats, and cargo vessels. A worldwide decline in commercial shipping in the 1980s, however, hurt Greek shipbuilding.

Agriculture

Once the most important sector of the Greek economy, agriculture now ranks second to manufacturing. A third of the land is suitable for crops, with another 40 percent used for pasture. Although large agricultural estates exist in Thrace and Macedonia, most of the country's farms are small. Poor soil and a dry summer climate also hinder agricultural production

from other countries is increasing, Greek textiles and cloth remain important exports. Demand for housing and an abundance of natural building materials have helped the construction industry to ex-

Shipbuilding and overseas trade have been important Greek industries since the end of World War II. At this yard, workers use dry docks, cranes, and scaffolding to build new cargo ships.

On this estate, a farmer dries the family's tobacco crop along the sunny side of their house. Tobacco, which is grown mostly in northern Greece, remains one of the country's principal crops.

in many parts of Greece. The Greek government has encouraged irrigation projects and the formation of cooperatives to increase production. Owners of some smaller farms have combined their holdings into larger and more efficient operations.

Wheat, corn, and barley are the country's most important grains. In northern Greece, some farmers cultivate rice. Tobacco, a common and profitable crop, is grown for export as well as for domestic use. Cotton fields supply the Greek textile

53

Workers ride a power shovel into a coal mine. Heavy equipment has increased the production of many Greek mines by making it easier to dig for valuable minerals.

industry. Farmers raise fruits and vegetables—including oranges, potatoes, tomatoes, grapes, and olives—on smaller acreages. Greece is one of the world's leading producers of lemons and raisins.

Pork and poultry are the country's most important meat sources. Some farmers raise beef cattle, but Greece lacks the well-watered grasslands needed by large cattle herds. More suited to the country's terrain are sheep and goats. Overgrazing by these animals, however, has damaged many rural pastures and has left large areas barren and unproductive.

Mining and Fishing

In recent years, Greece has increased the mining and processing of its extensive mineral resources. The country supplies many EC countries with the raw ores needed to make finished metals and other products.

Coal from the Peloponnesus, from Macedonia, and from Euboea fuels plants that generate electricity throughout Greece. Bauxite mines provide factories with the raw material to make aluminum. Workers quarry limestone, marble, and magnesite—common building materials—for the construction industry. Other mines produce iron ore, nickel, salt, zinc, lead, and sulfur. Greece also has developed offshore natural gas and petroleum deposits near the island of Thasos in the northern Aegean.

Overfishing and pollution have led to a sharp decline in Greece's fishing industry. Fishing crews still haul in mullet, tuna,

Greece's large domestic fishing fleet supplies shops in Greek cities with fresh seafood.

and sardines, which are sold mostly within the country. Sponges remain the principal marine export. Piraeus, Kavala in Thrace, and Thessaloniki are the largest fishing ports. Many coastal harbors and islands on the Aegean and Ionian Seas support small fleets of private fishing vessels. Commercial boats also fish the waters off the western coast of Africa.

Photo by Drs. A. A. M. van der Heyden, Naarden, the Netherlands

Courtesy of Minneapolis Public Library and Information Center

Small, private fishing operations still thrive in many Greek ports. These fishermen unload a day's catch from their nets onto the docks.

Trade and Shipping

Foreign trade—as a source of income, machinery, and food—remains a vital part of the Greek economy. The nation's most important trading partner is Germany, which is Greece's largest source of imports and biggest market for exports. Italy, France, and Britain are other important EU trading partners. Greece exports tobacco, cotton, dried fruits, textiles, clothing, and unprocessed minerals.

Greece has a large trade deficit, meaning that the country buys much more from other nations than it sells abroad. Crucial imports include machinery, transportation equipment, chemicals, red meat, dairy products, and petroleum.

Commercial cargo shipping has been a busy Greek industry since the end of World War II. With one of the world's largest merchant fleets, private Greek companies transport food, oil, and other

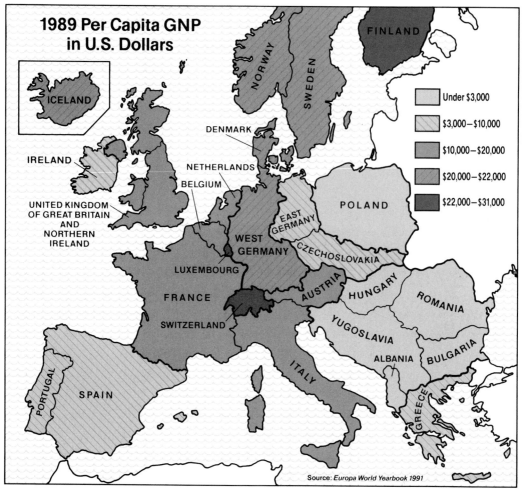

1989 Per Capita GNP in U.S. Dollars

Under $3,000
$3,000–$10,000
$10,000–$20,000
$20,000–$22,000
$22,000–$31,000

Source: *Europa World Yearbook 1991*

Artwork by Laura Westlund

This map compares the average productivity per person—calculated by gross national product (GNP) per capita—for 26 European nations. The GNP is the value of all goods and services produced by a nation in a year. To arrive at the GNP per capita, each nation's total GNP is divided by its population. The resulting dollar amount is one measure of the standard of living in each country. Greece's 1992–1994 figure of $7,710 puts the country among Europe's poorer nations. (Data taken from *Europa World Yearbook, 1991*.)

Completed in the late nineteenth century, the Corinth Canal eases the passage of ships from Athens and the Aegean Sea to the Ionian Sea off Greece's western coast. Before the canal was built, ships had to take a longer and more dangerous route around the headlands of the Peloponnesus.

Passenger and cargo ships crowd the Kantheros, or Great Harbor, of Piraeus. The Kantheros is the largest of three separate harbors within the city. Surrounding Piraeus is a busy manufacturing zone with factories, cotton mills, and metal foundries.

Photo by Ioannis Epaminondas

Completed in 406 B.C., the Erechtheion in Athens suffered extensive damage from wars, from invading armies, and from storms. In the early twentieth century, archaeologists completely rebuilt the exterior of this temple, which sits on the north side of the Acropolis.

products for businesses in many foreign countries. Most commercial ships use the port of Piraeus as their base. Fees from licenses and from the use of port facilities are an important source of income for the Greek government.

Tourism

Tourism has been growing in Greece since the 1970s, when agriculture declined and manufacturing suffered from foreign competition and inefficiency. The government built new hotels and other tourist facilities in undeveloped areas to lessen overcrowding and to spread the benefits of tourism to more remote areas of the country. Tourism is now a leading industry, although arrivals decline sharply whenever political turmoil occurs in southern Europe or in the Middle East.

The sunny climate and natural beauty of Greece attract millions of travelers each

Photo by Drs. A. A. M. van der Heyden, Naarden, the Netherlands

Visitors to Athens inspect sponges that vendors offer for sale on a busy market street.

After arriving at the main wharf of Santorini, tourists must climb a steep and winding path, either by foot or by donkey, to reach the town of Thira.

year. Delphi, Olympia, the ruins of the Acropolis, and a vast archaeological museum in Athens are the most popular sites for visitors. Developers have prepared new seaside resorts, golf courses, and skiing facilities. Island beaches and villages have become popular destinations for many northern Europeans. Private yachts and cruise ships sail the Ionian and Aegean seas. In the early 1990s, more than eight million tourists spent a total of about $2 billion each year in Greece. Tourism also is an important source of foreign money for banks and some private businesses.

Energy and Transportation

An extensive program sponsored by the government in the 1950s and 1960s brought electricity to many of Greece's remote and isolated areas. All major towns and cities and most rural villages now have electrical service. Coal-burning plants generate much of the country's power. New hydro-electric stations on the Achelous River in the Pindus Mountains supply energy to much of northern Greece.

After World War II, Greece upgraded its 25,000-mile network of roads. Workers widened and paved many routes that connect rural towns. Road travel within the country remains difficult, however, with high mountain ranges and narrow valleys hindering new construction.

Greece has 1,500 miles of public railroads that run along the Aegean coast of the mainland and in the Peloponnesus. Greece also has rail links with Bulgaria, the republic of Macedonia, and Turkey. A large public bus company provides transportation to remote locations that railroads do not reach.

Independent Picture Service

Since World War II, Greece has built several hydroelectric installations. Large dams are now generating electricity for isolated villages that did not previously have electric power.

Hydrofoils are the only link to the outside world for many of Greece's smaller inhabited islands. The residents of the islands depend on these boats for mail, for needed machinery, and for food supplies.

Passenger ferries connect inhabited islands to ports on the Greek mainland. Many of the smaller islands rely on these boats to bring in food, heavy equipment, and mail. International ferries call at the port of Igoumenitsa on the Ionian Sea, at Patras, and at Piraeus. Olympic Airlines, the national airline, flies to international and domestic destinations. The largest of the country's 20 airports is at Athens, and a new international airport is planned for the suburbs south of the capital.

An electric railway passes the ruins of the Theseion, an ancient Athenian temple. The railway begins in central Athens and travels to Piraeus.

Photo by Daniel H. Condit

A railroad and main highway run along the rugged cliffs between Corinth and Athens. Because of the mountainous terrain in many parts of Greece, important routes often must follow the seacoast.

Photo by Bruce Berg/Visuals Unlimited

This shop in Corfu offers fresh fruit and vegetables, as well as pet songbirds, for sale to the island's residents.

The Future

Greece occupies an important location at the crossroads of Europe and Asia. International conflicts taking place in the southern Mediterranean, in the Balkan countries, and in the Middle East often bring attention to Greece and to its foreign policy. But despite Greece's strategic importance to NATO, the country's leaders pursue an independent course in international disputes. The Greek government has negotiated the closing of two U.S. military bases on Greek soil. Greece also has an old and bitter dispute with Turkey, an allied NATO member, over the status of the divided island of Cyprus.

The Greeks brought the first flowering of art, literature, and science to the European continent. Greek leaders also developed the earliest western democracy, in which citizens held responsibility for their

Although civil marriage (marriage performed by a judge) was legalized in the 1980s, most Greek weddings are still performed within the Greek Orthodox Church.

own government. Yet in the early 1990s, after a tumultuous and violent history, Greeks are still seeking badly needed political stability.

Because Greek governments change so often, the country's economic development has suffered. Greece's continuing dependence on oil imports, as well as tourism, also makes the country's future uncertain. But membership in a unified EU market brings a chance in the coming decades for new trade opportunities, foreign investment, and economic growth.

Photo by Drs. A. A. M. van der Heyden, Naarden, the Netherlands

Photo by Ioannis Epaminondas

On the island of Thasos, residents line the streets for a glimpse of a passing carnival parade. The carnival season, which precedes the Greek Orthodox Easter, is an occasion for feasting, dancing, processions, and public ceremonies.

Index

Achelous River, 11, 60
Acropolis, 16, 22, 45, 58, 60
Aegean Sea, 5, 7-10, 12, 15, 17, 20, 57, 60
Agriculture, 9-11, 18-19, 21-22, 29, 36, 52-54, 58
Air travel, 61
Albania, 7-8, 35, 39
Alexander the Great, 23-24, 44
Alpheios River, 11
Architecture, 22, 45
Aristotle, 44
Asia, 22-24, 26, 29, 43, 62
Asia Minor, 5, 21-23, 26, 29, 33, 43
Athens, 9, 12, 15-17, 21-23, 25-26, 29, 34-35, 40, 42-43, 45-46, 50-52, 57-58, 60-62
Athens, University of, 17, 42
Athos, Mount, 6
Attica, 8-9, 15-16, 20, 39
Axios River, 11
Balkan Peninsula, 7, 17, 26, 29, 35, 37
Birthrate, 41
Boeotia, 8-9
Bulgaria, 7, 11, 33, 39, 60
Byzantine Empire, 17, 26-28, 44
Chios, 10
Christianity, 25-26, 45
Civil war, 35-36
Cleisthenes, 22
Climate, 11-13
Communist party, 34-35
Constantine, 25
Constantine I, 33-34
Constantinople, 25-29
Constitution, 30-31, 36-38
Corfu, 9
Corinth, 21-22, 25, 57, 62
Corinth, Gulf of, 8
Crete, 7, 10, 14, 18-21, 27, 31-33, 45
Crusaders, 27-28
Cyclades Islands, 9, 19-20, 21, 31
Cyprus, 37, 62
Delphi, 19, 22, 41, 60
Dodecanese Islands, 9, 30, 39
Dorians, 21
Eastern Orthodox Church, 27, 29, 45
Economy, 6, 15, 17, 32-34, 36-37, 39, 50-63
Education, 32, 42
El Greco. See Theotokopoulos, Domenikos
Emigration, 6, 39
Energy, 15, 50-51, 60
Environmental concerns, 15, 17, 54
Epirus, 8, 19, 32-33, 39, 49
Ethnic identity, 39
Euboea, 9, 15, 28, 54
Euboea, Gulf of, 9
European Union (EU), 6, 37, 50-51, 54, 56, 63
Eurotas River, 11
Exports, 18, 52-56
Festivals, 22, 46-47, 63
Fish and fishing, 15, 54-55
Flora and fauna, 13-15
Food, 47-48
France, 27, 29-30, 33-34, 51, 56
Franks, 26
George II, 33-35
Germany, 33-35, 56

Government, 38, 62-63
Great Britain, 29-31, 33-34, 56
Greece
    boundaries, size, and location of, 7
    flag of, 36
    future outlook of, 6, 38, 62-63
    independence of, 29-31
    population of, 39
Greek Orthodox Church, 41, 45-46, 62-63
Greek War of Independence, 17, 29-30
Gross national product (GNP), 56
Health, 17, 41-42
History, 19-38
    ancient Greece, 19-23
    Athens and Sparta, 23-24
    Byzantine Empire, 26-28
    independence, 29-33
    Ottoman rule, 28-30
    recent, 37-38
    Roman rule, 24-26
    world wars, 33-36
Homer, 43
Hydra, 7, 39
Icons, 45
Ida, Mount, 10
Iliad, The, 43
Imports, 50, 56
India, 23
Industry, 9, 17, 32, 36, 50-52, 54
Infant mortality, 41
Ionian Islands, 9, 28-29, 31
Ionian Sea, 7-8, 11, 15, 57, 60-61
Iraklion, 18
Islam, 46
Italy, 22, 26, 30, 34-35, 56
Ithaca, 9
Jews, 46
Judicial system, 38
Justinian, 26
Kalymnos, 9-10
Kapodistrias, Count Ioannis, 30-31
Karamanlis, Constantine, 36-37
Knights of St. John, 26
Knossos, 20
Kolokotronis, Theodore, 29
Kos, 9
Laconia, Gulf of, 11
Land, 7-17
Language, 23, 26, 39-41
Larissa, 18
Latin Empire, 27-28
Lesbos, 10, 43
Life expectancy, 42
Literacy, 42
Literature, 43-44
Lycabettus, 16
Macedonia (region), 8, 11, 15, 17, 23, 27, 29, 32-33, 52, 54
Macedonia (republic), 7, 11, 37, 60
Manufacturing, 17-18, 51-52
Marathon, Battle of, 22
Marathon Dam, 15
Mediterranean Sea, 7, 18, 20, 22, 24-25, 29, 37
Metaxas, General Ioannis, 34
Middle East, 21, 23, 25-28, 52, 58, 62
Military junta, 36-37
Minerals and mining, 15, 54, 56
Minoans, 20-21
Minos, King, 20
Mitsotakis, Constantine, 37-38

Mycenaeans, 21
Mykonos, 9, 11
National Archaeological Museum, 17, 60
Natural resources, 15, 39, 50-51
Navarino, Battle of, 30
Naxos, 9
New Democracy party, 37-38
Normans, 26-27
North Africa, 19, 21, 26-28
North Atlantic Treaty Organization (NATO), 35, 62
Northern Cyprus, Republic of, 37
Odyssey, The, 43
Oil, 15, 51, 56, 63
Olives, 6, 9-10, 14, 52, 54
Olympia, 11, 60
Olympic Games, 3, 11, 22, 49
Olympus, Mount, 9
Otto I, 31
Ottoman Empire, 29-31
Ottoman Turks, 5, 16-18, 28-31, 33
Paleologus, Michael, 28
Papadopoulos, Colonel Georgios, 36
Papandreou, Andreas, 37-38
Papandreou, Georgios, 36
Parliament 31, 34, 38
Parnassus, Mount, 19, 49
Parthenon, 45
PASOK, 37-38
Patmos, 2, 10
Patras, 17-18, 61
Patras, Gulf of, 8, 11
Peloponnesian War, 23, 43
Peloponnesus, 8, 11-13, 15, 17, 21, 28, 30-31, 39, 54, 57, 60
People, 39-49
Pericles, 23
Persian Empire, 22-23
Philosophy, 23, 43-44
Pindus Mountains, 8, 11-13, 60
Pinios River, 10-11
Pinios River Valley, 19
Piraeus, 16, 55, 57-58, 61
Plato, 44
Population, 16-18, 39
Ports, 9, 16-18, 21, 55, 57-58, 61
Railways, 32, 60-61
Recreation, 49
Republicans, 34
Rhodes, 9, 12, 14, 26, 28, 44
Rivers, 10-11
Roads and highways, 8, 10, 32, 60, 62
Roman Catholic Church, 27, 45-46
Roman Empire, 16, 25-26
Royalists, 34-35
Russia, 29-30
Samos, 10
Samothrace, 10
Santorini, 9, 21, 45, 59
Saronic Gulf, 9, 16
Sculpture, 3, 20-22, 44-45
Shipping, 8, 17-18, 52, 56-58
Sicily, 22
Simitis, Konstantinos, 38
Socialist party (PASOK), 37-38
Socrates, 43-44
Sounion, Cape, 8
Sparta, 11, 16, 21, 23
Sponges, 2, 15, 55, 58
Sporades, 10
Sports, 22, 48-49

Strymon River, 11
Textiles, 17-18, 52-54, 56
Thasos, 10, 50, 54
Thebes, 21
Theotokopoulos, Domenikos (El Greco), 45
Thermaic Gulf, 11
Thessaloniki, 11-12, 17, 26, 33, 37, 46, 51, 55
Thessaly, 9-11, 18-19, 21, 32
Thrace, 8, 10-11, 33, 39, 52, 55
Tobacco, 18, 51, 53, 56
Topography, 7-10
Tourism, 7, 11, 17-18, 20, 49, 58-60, 63
Trade, 6, 20-22, 24, 29, 37, 50, 56, 63
Transportation, 7, 60-62
Turkey, 5, 7-10, 16-17, 21, 29-34, 37, 60, 62
Turkish Cypriots, 37
Unemployment, 34, 50
United States, 35-36, 51, 62
Venizelos, Eleutherios, 32-34
Villehardouin, Geoffrey de, 28
Vikings, 26
Visual arts, 44-45
Volos, 18
Volos, Gulf of, 9
Voting rights, 35-36, 38
William George, Prince (George I), 31
World War I, 33-34
World War II, 34-36, 46, 60
Ypsilanti, Alexander, 29-30
Yugoslavia, 37
Zakynthos, 9